The Y'shua Challenge

Answers for Those Who Say Jews Can't Believe in Jesus

PART I

A Purple Pomegranate Booklet
Purple Pomegranate Productions
San Francisco, California

The Y'shua Challenge, Part 1
Answers to those who say Jews can't believe in Jesus
©1993
by Purple Pomegranate Productions
80 Page Street, San Francisco, CA 94102

First Edition
All rights reserved. For reprint permission, please write
to Purple Pomegranate Productions, Permissions Depart-
ment, 80 Page Street, San Francisco, CA 94102.

Cover design and art by Pavel Bosak
Compiled by Eliyah Gould, Rich Robinson and
Ruth Rosen

ISBN 1-881022-03-X

All Scripture quoted, unless otherwise noted, is from the
Holy Bible, New King James Version. Copyright 1979,
1980 and 1982 by Thomas Nelson Publishers. Used by
permission.

Printed in the United States of America

Introduction

It's been observed that most Jewish people don't believe in Jesus. Some people conclude that such disbelief is a contrary stubbornness in the face of evidence. That is unfair and untrue thinking!

Most Jewish people, even most rabbis, have not turned their backs on the evidence for Jesus—they've simply never gotten in the courtroom to hear the evidence and to see the exhibits. The conclusions they've drawn are based on hearsay.

If Jesus is the Messiah, you can bet that the Jewish people are the first who would want to know about it; the Jewish people would benefit the most if Jesus is our Messiah.

This booklet launches a series of essays called *The Y'shua Challenge*. It is written by Jewish believers in Jesus to our fellow Jews who don't yet believe in him. If you are not Jewish, but are interested in Jews, Jesus, and Jewish thoughts, welcome to the forum!

If these essays accomplish as much as we hope, it will be a miracle, and that's not a facetious statement! You see, the writers of The Y'shua Challenge believe in miracles—and that is just what it may take for some readers to grasp for themselves what we have discovered about Y'shua (Jesus).

It may sound presumptuous to declare what "we have discovered" when most of the Jewish community, in fact, most of the world, doesn't see what we see in Y'shua. We **don't** think that we are so smart and everyone else is so stupid. It's just that some people choose to investigate the person and purpose of Y'shua, and others elect to shut their hearts and minds to any thought that his claims might be true.

Various religions attempt to explain Y'shua in different ways. The Hindu religion sees Jesus as one of many gods. The Muslim religion admits, remarkably, that Jesus was sent from God; yet it concludes that he was only one among many holy prophets.

Perhaps most important of all, the Jewish religion challenges the messiahship of Jesus. This challenge is preeminent, because, after all, we, Jewish people, were the ones expecting the Messiah. It was our prophets who spoke of his coming. Jesus came as a Jew to the Jewish people, yet he came to benefit all people everywhere who would trust him. If Jesus is the Messiah, as he claimed to be, our response to him is vital—because it is not merely a response to him but to God's promise.

Automatic Response

Many Jewish people dismiss Jesus without much thought, regarding him as being only for non-Jews. This is because the word *Christian* has been mistakenly used as—and believed to be—a synonym for *gentile.* (Not all gentiles are Christians, and not all Christians are gentiles.) Most Jews know that the concept of the Messiah is a Jewish doctrine, but many do not realize that *Christ* is simply a non-Jewish, Greek-based translation of the word *Messiah,* or *Mashiach.* That means that gentiles who believe in Christ believe in the Jewish Messiah.

The question is not really whether Jews should believe in Jesus, but whether anyone, Jewish or gentile, should. While this booklet is addressed largely to Jewish readers, we hope that gentiles will also accept the challenge of Y'shua. If he is not the Messiah, then he is not what he claimed to be, and no one should believe in him.

4

Rabbis or Jewish scholars would never presume to tell non-Jews that they should not believe in Jesus. However, within the Jewish community, our people are indoctrinated early in life to believe that Y'shua is not the Messiah and that he is not for us. The messiahship of Jesus has been challenged by many of our religious leaders almost from the beginning. His claims are still being challenged today.

The Objections

Those challenges are either tenable or untenable, and the thoughtful Jew or gentile ought to deal with them, test them, and see if the arguments hold water. We've taken a few sample arguments against the messiahship of Jesus to show that there are answers. One small booklet like this one cannot possibly answer all the challenges. More *Y'shua Challenge* questions and answers will be available to people interested in further investigation.

Most of the questions and objections we address are not new; many were codified by Isaac Ben Abraham Troki, a Jewish scholar who lived c. 1533–c. 1594. Troki's book, *Hizzuk Emunah* (meaning "faith strengthened"), contains objections to Christianity that strengthened and fortified those Jewish people who did not want to discover that Jesus was the Messiah.[1] Such people could, if they desired, repeat the objections and challenges from Troki's book without stopping to investigate whether or not his claims were true.

That does not mean they sought to believe an untruth. Most who repeated Troki's arguments simply wanted to be loyal to the Jewish people. Troki's book helped them affirm the decision that all sincere Jews are expected to make about Jesus: that he is not for us.

5

This booklet focuses on one set of objections: that through their character and actions, Y'shua's followers prove that he is not the Messiah. You may have heard (and perhaps you've even said) that a Jew would have to be a meshuggener or a meshumad (a crazy person or a traitor) to believe in Jesus. Most likely you are neither, so given that premise, Y'shua is not for you. If, however, the premise is flawed, then maybe you should not dismiss him without making sincere inquiries.

Everyone Is Welcome

Are you willing to risk making the discovery that Y'shua might actually be for you? Would you weigh the answers to some of the challenges? Will you hear from Jews who believe that Jesus brought the best possible news—a message that ought not be missed? Will you consider who Jesus is?

God does not deal with people in national or ethnic blocks. He speaks, beckons, calls out to each of us and challenges us to make the right choice, to respond wisely to the person of Y'shua. The question is, are we willing to consider and meet the challenge that the Almighty Creator has set before us?

Since you have read this far, you are probably an open-minded person. You are probably curious, and you are not afraid to read something different.

Even if you are skeptical, and if the mention of open-mindedness makes you uncomfortable, please don't stop reading. Y'shua left plenty of room for skeptics! He said, "Ask, and it will be given to you; seek, and you will find; knock, and it will be opened to you. For everyone who asks receives, he who seeks finds, and to him who knocks it will be opened." (Luke 11:9–10)

True skeptics are willing to approach a subject without a predisposition to reject what they hear before trying it in the crucibles of their own knowledge. True skeptics seek wisdom before making a commitment to belief or disbelief.

On the other hand, if you are a committed cynic and already "know" that Jesus couldn't possibly be the Messiah, the remainder of this booklet will only encourage you. It will prove that you are right! Cynics approach responses to objections with the knowledge that those responses won't make any difference. Cynics will read for the sole purpose of finding flaws and faults in a given case. If that describes you, doubtless you will find the flaws and faults you seek, even if they are not there. Yet we welcome cynics. There is always the possibility that you will catch a glimpse of something or someone more worthy of your commitment, for cynicism truly is a commitment.

The Challenge

Perhaps this booklet will help you see that many objections raised about Y'shua are questionable. Our hope is that you will begin to look past some of those questionable objections as you face the challenge of how to respond to Y'shua. Whether you consider yourself a seeker, a skeptic or a cynic, maybe you are someone who would really want to know the truth about Jesus if you thought it could be known.

If you can allow yourself to be open to discovering whatever God might have for your life, why not take a moment before you turn the page to ask him to help you discern if what you will find in this booklet is true.

Answers
for Those Who Say
Jews Can't Believe
in Jesus

Before we go any further, please make a mental list of reasons you have either heard or formulated for thinking Jews should not believe in Y'shua. How many of those reasons actually regard Jesus? How many concern his followers rather than himself?

The objections to Jesus' followers (both Jewish and gentile) are vast! They reach back to his followers in the first century C.E. and stretch forward to present-day believers. But these objections shift the focus away from Y'shua. By making believers in Jesus the focal point, people don't have to deal with the challenge of Jesus himself. They dismiss the messengers so that they don't need to accept or reject the message.

A Net of Objections
The objections (many of which are actually accusations) might be seen as a kind of net designed to surround and isolate—to keep Y'shua's followers from influencing the rest of the world, particularly the Jewish world.

You might suppose that this net of objections was designed to immobilize the followers of Y'shua. But allow yourself to consider what we Jewish believers in

Jesus see when we look at the net of objections: We see those who are afraid to consider the gospel message huddled beneath the net! The net seems to be intended as a safety device to keep people from wandering into what some consider "dangerous territory." Several emotionally charged strands of the net prevent anyone from coming too close to what the followers öf Y'shua have to say. Do you see how it works? Even if people are curious about Y'shua, they cannot approach the subject without asking, "How can I even consider their message when blank and blank and blank," and each blank points to one of the accusations against the followers of Jesus. The net keeps individuals in a place where they can't listen to what they have been made to feel they should not hear.

Yet people still have a choice. The net of objections is loosely woven, even riddled with holes—gaps of logic as well as missing facts.

The major strands of the net of objections to Jesus' followers are:

1. First century followers of Y'shua (particularly the Apostle Paul) invented a new religion, never intended by Jesus, based on theology he would have completely rejected.

2. Jesus' first-century followers planted seeds of anti-Semitism, and Christians have continued to bear the bitter fruit of hatred and violence.

3. Jewish people who join the ranks of those followers are no longer Jews. Their expressions of Jewish identity and use of Jewish symbols are therefore fraudulent.

4. Since accepting Christian beliefs means a person is no longer Jewish, any Jew who does so is either deceived by sneaky tactics, deficient in decision-making abilities or simply doesn't like being Jewish.

10

5. All of the above implies that Jews who invite other Jews to believe in Jesus are even worse because they are leading other Jews to become "disloyal" like them.

It seems fair to ask, are the objections raised about Jesus' followers true? Do they warrant a dismissal of Jesus? Many assume that the answer to both questions is yes. But without pertinent information, that assumption comes dangerously close to prejudice, which does not help anyone. Therefore we appreciate your willingness to read the following challenge to this net of objections.

Blame It on Paul

First, let us consider the idea that Christianity was invented by Jesus' followers (particularly by the Apostle Paul).

Paul has been accused of intentionally distorting the teachings of Jesus in order to make Christianity more appealing to the gentiles. What information exists to prove or disprove this theory?

It seems fair to presume that one cannot claim Jesus' teachings were distorted without first knowing what Jesus taught. Do those who claim distortion demonstrate knowledge of Jesus' teachings? People who accuse Paul of creating a new religion usually say that Jesus never claimed to be the Messiah, nor did he claim to be the son of God. Many repeat that allegation without ever having read Jesus' teachings. One need only read the first four books of the New Testament (not written by Paul) to see the invalidity of this objection.[2] For example, consider the following account from the perspective of Matthew: When Jesus came into the region of Caesarea Philippi, he asked his disciples, saying "Who do men say the Son of Man is?"[3]

11

So they said, "Some say John the Baptist, some say Elijah, and others Jeremiah or one of the prophets."

But he said to them, "who do you say that I am?"

And Simon Peter answered and said, "You are the Christ [Messiah], the Son of the living God."

Jesus replied, "Blessed are you, Simon Bar Jonah, for flesh and blood has not revealed this to you, by man, but my Father who is in heaven." (Matthew 16:13-17; NIV)

This is one of many references that show who Jesus claimed to be. The assertion that Paul invented a role that Jesus never took for himself is not only insupportable, but anyone can easily obtain information to the contrary.

However, the claims Y'shua made of himself do not necessarily negate other accusations against the Apostle Paul. Perhaps you have heard some of them:

• Paul's teachings were derived from Greek paganism and mystery religions.

• Paul wasn't really Jewish

• Paul was sneaky and deceitful.

Paul's Big Idea

Detractors most commonly ascribe doctrines such as the deity of Jesus, the resurrection, sacramental meals and baptism to pagan origins. Again, if you'll investigate the sources, you'll see each of these doctrines or events is recorded in the first four books of the New Testament, not written by Paul. Two of the four writers were some of Jesus' closest associates. In addition, most of these things were not alien to the Jewish thought or practice of Jesus' day.

Resurrection was a belief strongly held by the Pharisees, and it is still affirmed daily by observant Jews who recite the Thirteen Articles of Faith. Jesus

12

himself instituted them at a Passover celebration.[4]

John the Baptist, Jesus' forerunner, practiced **baptism** long before Paul was on the scene.[5] Throngs of Jewish people came to be immersed in water; no doubt they were accustomed to the idea of baptism because of the Jewish ritual of mikvah.

In light of these facts, it is perplexing that scholars such as Samuel Levine claim that Paul "introduced a few pagan myths into the new Christian religion so that it would appeal to the pagan Gentiles."[6]

The New Testament accounts of the early church reveal that things happened precisely the other way around. According to Acts 15, early Jewish Christian church leaders were not seeking to entice gentiles into following Jesus, but rather were prohibiting them from participating because of their pagan background. Some even demanded the new gentile Christians to be circumcised and to live as Torah observant Jews.

It was not Paul, but Peter and James who advocated for leniency concerning those gentile believers in Jesus.

"Therefore I [James] judge that we should not trouble those from among the Gentiles who are turning to God, but that we write to them to abstain from things polluted by idols, from sexual immorality, from things strangled, and from blood." (Acts 15:19-20)

This was agreeable to the other church leaders, including Paul. Nowhere is it recorded that Paul or any other Jewish Christian ever suggested for any reason that belief in Jesus should be mixed with pagan rituals.

Despite the lack of evidence, many accept claims about the non-Jewish nature of Paul's teaching without question, seemingly out of loyalty to Judaism. Yet some scholarly works question and challenge those

13

claims. One such current writing is W. D. Davies' ground-breaking book, *Paul and Rabbinic Judaism: Some Rabbinic Elements in Pauline Theology* (1948).

How Jewish Was Paul?

A person is either Jewish or not Jewish, and few actually believe that Paul was not. Hyam Maccoby is virtually alone in his opinion that Paul was a gentile.[7] However, if we can speak of the extent to which one demonstrates Jewish identity as that person's "Jewishness," perhaps it is Paul's Jewishness that people wish to call into question.

Perhaps most telling is what Paul himself had to say about being Jewish. Here is how he described himself: "Circumcised the eighth day, of the stock of Israel, of the tribe of Benjamin, a Hebrew of the Hebrews; concerning the law, a Pharisee; concerning zeal, persecuting the church; concerning the righteousness which is in the law, blameless." (Philippians 3:5–6)

What did it mean to be "a Hebrew of the Hebrews"? *Hebrews* was a specialized term that referred to Jews who spoke Aramaic and worshiped at Hebrew-speaking congregations, as opposed to *Hellenists* who spoke and worshiped in Greek. A Hebrew of the Hebrews indicates an Aramaic-speaking, observant Jew whose parents were also Hebrews. Hebrews outside the land in places such as Tarsus—a city located in what today is Turkey—were immigrants who kept the more observant lifestyle of their place of origin.[8]

Paul also wrote: "I am indeed a Jew, born in Tarsus of Cilicia, but brought up in this city [Jerusalem] at the feet of Gamaliel, I taught according to the strictness of our fathers' law, and was zealous toward God as you all are today." (Acts 22:3)

14

Paul was educated at the feet of one of the most eminent Pharisaic rabbis of his time. In those days, leading rabbis headed schools in which they taught their perspectives and views to disciples. Gamaliel either succeeded the famous Hillel as head of the school of Hillel or headed his own school.[9] He sat on the Sanhedrin, the Supreme Court of ancient Israel, and had a reputation of great piety. The Mishnah[10] states: "When Rabban Gamaliel the Elder died, the glory of the Law ceased and purity and separateness died." The Pharisees were the separated ones. This accolade was tantamount to saying that Gamaliel was the last, and perhaps the best, exemplar of Pharisaism.

Of course, some may argue that Paul received his training before he became a follower of Jesus. What can we know of his Jewishness afterward?

Priority of Jewishness

In his letter to the Romans, Paul described his anguish over the disbelief of many fellow Jews: "I have great sorrow and continual grief in my heart. For I could wish that I myself were accursed from Christ for my brethren, my kinsmen according to the flesh." (Romans 9:2,3)

The Book of Romans was written to gentile, as well as Jewish, believers in Jesus. In this book Paul expressed his deep identification with the Jewish people, to the point of willingness to sacrifice his own relationship with God for the sake of his fellow Jews. He also made a point of emphasizing the value of Jewish heritage and identity: "Israelites, to whom pertain the adoption, the glory, the covenants, the giving of the law, the service of God, and the promises; of whom are the fathers and from whom, according to the flesh, Christ came, who is over all, the eternally

15

blessed God. Amen." (Romans 9:4–5)

Two chapters later, Paul warns gentile believers in Jesus not to be conceited or arrogant toward the Jewish people. As for God's attitude toward the people of Israel, Paul asks and answers the question: "I say then, has God cast away his people? Certainly not! For I also am an Israelite, of the seed of Abraham, of the tribe of Benjamin." (Romans 11:1)

We can also see how crucial Jewishness was to Paul, inasmuch as he circumcised Timothy, his apprentice, before allowing him along on a preaching tour. Timothy's mother was Jewish, and his father was Greek. While Paul spoke against **forced** gentile circumcision, he felt it was important for Timothy to be circumcised. Paul wanted to be certain that the Jewish people they encountered realized that though Timothy's father was Greek, Timothy had chosen to identify with his mother's people. [11]

Paul's Personality: Deceptive or Deferential?

Paul has been charged with deceit as he proclaimed the message of Y'shua.

In 1 Corinthians 9:20–22, he wrote: "To the Jews I became as a Jew, that I might win Jews; to those who are under the law, as under the law, that I might win those who are under the law; to those who are without law, as without law (not being without law toward God, but under law toward Christ), that I might win those who are without law; to the weak I became as weak, that I might win the weak. I have become all things to all men, that I might by all means save some."

Regarding this and other passages from Paul, anti-missionary author Beth Moshe says his writings "demonstrate the unreliability of the man who actually formulated the break away from Judaism by the early Church. . . . Now see who he is, by his own words. He admitted using trickery and deception to gain his ends."[12]

First Corinthians 9:20–22 is a favorite passage for those interested in dismissing the gospel message through discrediting the gospel messenger. However, the anti-missionary analysis seems to reflect more eagerness to find fault than to find the meaning of the passage.

David Daube, a Jewish legal scholar, wrote *The New Testament and Rabbinic Judaism* to illuminate the Jewish background of the New Testament. He gives an entirely different perspective on Paul's writing in 1 Corinthians:

"[This idea is] taken over by Paul from Jewish teaching on the subject: the idea that you must adopt the customs and mood of the person you wish to win over. . . .

"This attitude had formed part of Jewish missionary practice long before Paul. Two Talmudic illustrations of Hillel's work are relevant: he accepted into the fold a gentile who refused to acknowledge the oral Law, and he accepted another who refused to acknowledge any Law beyond the most fundamental ethical principle. . . . At the decisive moment of conversion, he fell in with the notions of the applicant and declared himself satisfied with recognition of the written Law or a single, basic moral precept. . . .

"Both Jewish and Christian circles which were desirous of proselytes, in approaching heathens, deliberately stressed the precepts concerning decency and good manners at the expense of levitical and theological ones. . . .

"Paul, when he wrote the passage from 1 Corinthians quoted at the beginning, was drawing on a living element in Jewish religion."[13]

To paraphrase Daube, Paul was not a practitioner of deceit any more than other Jewish leaders who simply utilized good teaching techniques.

Teaching techniques and missionary zeal notwithstanding, we ought to approach the text itself with some fairness. The passage in no way suggests hiding one's own identity in order to trick others. "Being all things to all people" does not imply deception. Contrary to the spin that detractors attempt to put on this passage, Paul never said, "I told Jews I am Jewish and I told gentiles I am gentile and I would tell anybody anything if it would make them believe in Jesus."

"I became as" means that Paul adapted his demeanor, behavior and expression. When Paul spoke to people, whether they were Jewish, gentile, weak, strong or whatever, he purposed that they would not be hindered by feelings of inferiority or superiority. Paul was able to meet and speak to all people as equals no matter what their position. He always actually was what he appeared to be—on the level with the person to whom he was speaking.

Those familiar with Paul's teachings and high ethical standards see his willingness to relate to others within their own context as an act of graciousness. To him, being all things to all people meant putting others first and not insisting on one's own rights or preferences if doing so hindered others from hearing the message of Y'shua. It meant deferring to the needs of others. This is in keeping with Paul's teachings to the Philippians:

"Let nothing be done through selfish ambition or conceit, but in lowliness of mind let each esteem others better than himself. Let each of you look out not only for his own interests, but also for the interests of others. Let this mind be in you which was also in Christ Jesus." (Philippians 2:3–5)

The objections to Paul as a sinister figure who sowed seeds of hatred against his own people and distorted Jesus' teachings to include pagan myths do not seem to hold water. Yet there are other, more formidable objections to Y'shua's followers.

Christians Persecute Jews

Persecution in the name of Jesus is the most emotionally charged strand of the net of objections. More than anything else, many people point to "Christian anti-Semitism" as a reason to dismiss Jesus. When Jewish people find themselves questioning whether Jesus might be the Messiah, thoughts of the Crusades and the Holocaust quickly rush to mind, setting off a warning signal—Jews who believe join the same league as those who hate our people. When Jewish people allow that signal to block any further contemplation of Jesus, they base their decisions not upon who Jesus is, but rather upon who they do not want to be (namely, among those who persecute Jews).

How can a Jewish believer respond to the accusation that we have joined the persecutors? Anti-Semitism is a fact that should never be minimized or pushed out of mind. Nor can we avoid the fact that many people have used the name of Jesus as a justification for their anti-Semitic crimes. **Yet we need to ask questions.** For example, can we truly blame our sufferings on Jesus and the things he taught? Can those who have wrongly used the name of Jesus make it wrong for us to believe and trust in him? Can the evil committed in Y'shua's name free us from the responsibility of considering his true identity? These

19

are important questions, because if the answer is no and we continue to allow anti-Semitism to prevent us from considering Jesus, **we allow anti-Semites to keep us in the dark about the greatest Jew who ever lived**—which produces an even greater injustice against us.

It is important to remember that Jesus never taught hatred of Jewish people, nor did that hatred begin with the church. Persecution was a fact of Jewish existence in the days of Pharaoh and Haman. People justify their hatred in various ways, and some of the worst sins committed are cloaked in false piety. It is human nature to justify ourselves, no matter how ugly our actions. To claim loyalty to a noble person or cause is the perfect justification for the worst possible crimes. Such associations (however false) enable people to deceive themselves into believing that their wicked deeds are righteous.

The French Revolution was a bloodbath in the name of liberty, fraternity and equality. But who would say that liberty, fraternity and equality are ideals to be despised because of that bloodshed? People have committed terrible acts in the name of freedom and justice, but that doesn't make freedom and justice wrong. Nor do we label everyone who advocates freedom and justice as murderers, even though so many criminals have attempted to justify their terrible deeds in the name of those noble causes.

Jesus and his teachings have no connection to crimes committed in his name.

How can we blame Jesus for those who claim to follow his teachings but do not? We might say that if he had never existed, no one could misuse his name, but that is like burying our heads in the sand. Jesus is not to blame for the misuse of his name. In the same way, how are those who wish to explain his teachings to be blamed for those who have distorted them? If (as some have done) we blame all believers in Jesus for killing people they never knew, we become guilty of the same thing our persecutors do when they wrongly blame all Jews for the crucifixion of Jesus.

What a frightening (but not unnatural) phenomenon it is when the wrongly judged and hated turn around and wrongly judge and hate others. It takes tremendous determination for those who have been persecuted not to persecute others in turn. We must remember not to do to others what we hate having done to ourselves. As Jesus put it, "And just as you want men to do to you, you also do to them likewise"(Luke 6:31).

The Holocaust

People often describe the Holocaust as the climax of 2,000 years of Christian mistreatment of Jews. Some invoke the Shoah as the ultimate reason for Jews not to believe in Jesus.

Jewish believer Moishe Rosen challenges that view: "The phrase '2,000 years of history leading up to the Holocaust' is more than a reference to past prejudice and persecution. It is an indictment against Christianity that misrepresents Christ's message and intent. Anyone who gives credence to such an accusation bestows upon Hitler the power to change theology."[14]

Neither Jesus nor Christian ideals produced the Holocaust. Those murders were generated by the same perversion of human nature that the holy Scriptures depict, beginning in the Book of Genesis. Cain turned on his own brother and became the first murderer. And while the Jewish people have been singled out more often for genocide than any other people, we are by no means the only group of people to be methodically murdered. Consider the "ethnic cleansing," the systematic rape and murder of the Bosnian people perpetrated in the 1990s. No, genocide neither began nor ended with Hitler and the Jewish people.

Some see the Holocaust not merely as an indictment against Christianity but against God. Many who suffered through the concentration camps either blame God or refuse to believe that he exists.

Such people find themselves in a quandary, ever restless until they know in what or in whom they can place their faith. Will they dismiss God on the grounds that the Holocaust proves him cruel, incapable or non-existent and instead put their faith in humanity? If God is not to be trusted because he permits humans to be cruel, does it make more sense to trust humans when it is human beings—not God—who have proved to be inescapably, or at least repeatedly, corrupt?

Often those who say they don't believe in God because of the terrible acts that have been committed actually try to punish God for what they see as his failure to prevent suffering. What can a person do to show his or her displeasure with God, other than refuse to acknowledge his existence? Yet it is we, not God, who suffer when we deny that he exists and that he cares.

Deep down, most of us realize that we need to have faith in someone or something more worthy of trust than ourselves. If God is "dead," then so, too, is humanity. If we had only each other or ourselves to depend upon, we would soon be reduced to cynical misanthropes.

How much better it is to have faith in the God of the Scriptures, who will see that ultimate justice prevails. Evil people who acted out their own hatred—not God, not Jesus—are to blame for the atrocities of the Holocaust.

Could it be that those who blame God or Jesus or Christianity simply can't bear the awful reality that since history began, human beings from all walks of life have demonstrated the potential to commit any horror imaginable?

Could it be that each person is capable of hatred and that we don't want to face that truth about ourselves?

Jesus called upon all he met, from every walk of life, to face their flawed nature and corrupt inclinations and repent of pride, prejudice and every other evil that can bear the fruit of violence.

It is horrendous that of all names, his has been used to accomplish the exact opposite of everything he instructed. How can we allow this obvious perversion to color our response to his teachings and his claims?

Could it be that blaming Jesus for the evils of the centuries is less painful than admitting the dark shadows that exist in every human heart?

There is no way we can undo the tragedy of the Holocaust. We have no control over what has already happened. We do, however, have the ability to prevent Hitler from continuing to reach us from beyond the grave.

Why should he have the power to prevent us from investigating who Y'shua is? He will only have that power if we give it to him.

The Use or Misuse of Symbols

Symbols (except those under copyright laws) are not owned like property. They are fluid, subject to

23

new uses and to re-interpretation. Yet Jews who believe in Jesus are often accused of misusing Jewish symbols, almost as though they were trespassing or stealing private property. The charge is that Jewish believers reinterpret Jewish symbols and use them to point to Jesus. Some people suggest that Jewish believers mislead people into thinking that a Jew can remain Jewish after embracing Jesus.

It is true that many Jewish believers in Y'shua use Jewish symbols. It is not true that they do so to deceive anyone into thinking they are Jewish when they are not. The fact is, according to Halakhah (Jewish Law), a person never stops being Jewish, even if he or she is an apostate.[15] Jewish believers might debate the term *apostate*, but even if they are apostates, that is no basis for saying they are no longer Jews. There is no deception involved when Jewish believers in Jesus maintain that they are still Jews, not only according to their own consciences, but also according to the Jewish Law.

Those who do not believe in Jesus certainly have every right to disagree with those who do, but Jewish identity cannot be revoked like a driver's license. When people say that one cannot be Jewish and believe in Jesus, it simply is not true.

If Jewish believers in Jesus truly were not Jewish, and knew they were not Jewish, but still claimed to be—that would be deceptive! However, we remain Jewish. By the same token, to tell others that they can accept Jesus as Messiah and remain Jews would only be deceptive if, in fact, they would no longer be Jews, which again, is not true.

When people accuse Jewish believers in Jesus of deception, they express impossible certainty about unknowable motives and intentions. Those who make such allegations would have to be omniscient to divine the driving force of all Jewish believers in Jesus. Could it be that the real deception lies in perpetrating the notion that Jews stop being Jewish when they believe in Jesus?

As for Jewish believers in Jesus reinterpreting Jewish symbols—how is this deceptive? When Y'shua celebrated Passover with his disciples, he made a spiritual application. He stated that the seder symbols were not only about the redemption from Egypt, but they also symbolized the sacrifice he was about to make.[16] He wanted to be remembered by his disciples in the Passover celebration. Jews who celebrate Passover in a way that points to Y'shua are following his example.

Jesus and his followers are certainly not the only Jewish people who have adapted symbols to changing situations. Jews have used the Passover freedom motif not only in its traditional Exodus setting but also in support of political freedom and freedom for Russian Jews.[17] Others have even used the Passover themes to incorporate New Age teachings.[18] You may support all or none of those causes. You may think the re-interpretations are good or bad. Even if you don't support them, you probably do not regard those who do as deceivers who contrive their re-interpretations to ensnare others.

The mezuzah is another example of a symbol whose meaning has been modified. According to Scripture and rabbinical tradition, a mezuzah is supposed to be affixed to the doorpost of the Jewish home. In the Bible, the mezuzah symbolized the fact that God's commandments were to be kept. Today many Jews wear them as pendants to symbolize their Jewish identity and nothing more. No doubt observant Jews frown upon using mezuzot as jewelry. However, Jews who wear them are not likely to be accused of deception even though they do not observe the Law the way a mezuzah seems to imply they should.

The Magen David, or Star of David, has also been adapted. Most Jews today accept the Magen David as an obviously Jewish symbol without thinking twice about its origins or history. Yet when the star began to be used widely in the nineteenth and early twentieth centuries, it was strongly opposed in some Jewish quarters. The poet Judah Leib Gordon objected to its use in the St. Petersburg synagogue because, he claimed, it originally was used by pagan Druids. Hungarian rabbi Leopold Löw, named "the century's greatest authority in the field," alleged the star was derived from German myths.[19]

Moritz Güdemann, writing in 1916, also objected: "Men of Jewish learning cannot accept the fact that the Jewish people would dig out of their attic of superstition a symbol or emblem that it shares with stables."[20]

Güdemann was Orthodox and anti-Zionist and was especially enraged over the use of the symbol for a Jewish flag.

How is this relevant to the use of Jewish symbols by today's Jewish believers in Jesus? Güdemann objected to the Jewish community's general use of a symbol that had been adopted by a movement he disdained.[21] Today's rabbis object to the use of that same symbol (now accepted as Jewish) by a movement they disdain. In both cases, people sought separation from that which they held in contempt.

The refusal to countenance the use of common symbolism is not about deception, it is

about distance. When people get angry about Jewish believers in Jesus using Jewish symbols, it is not because there is something dishonest afoot. Jews who believe in Jesus openly talk about their faith. They do not use Jewish symbols to hide their belief in Jesus; they use them to express the fact that they still value their Jewishness. The anger is due to the fact that Jewish believers in Jesus will not succumb to the demand that they distance themselves from their Jewishness. Apparently some people fear any contact with Jewish believers, therefore they advocate total separation.

If a person wants to say, "I don't like what you believe, and I don't want anything to do with you," we may feel sad, but that is his or her right, after all. But no one has a right to say, "I don't like what you believe and therefore I don't want you to have anything in common with me." People have a right to separate themselves from others. They don't, however, have a right to separate others from their own personal heritage and the expression of their own identity. Jews cannot be excommunicated by other Jews.

The question arises: Can those who declare Jewish believers in Jesus unacceptable expect to be received as authorities on how those they reject may or may not express themselves?

Ironically, these "authorities" often accuse Jewish believers in Jesus of turning their backs on their people, culture and Jewish identity in general. Paradoxically, when those same Jewish believers maintain any kind of demonstrable Jewish identity, often they are accused of fraudulence. If they considered themselves non-Jews, they would have no interest in Jewish symbols.

27

All of this raises some questions you might ponder:

•Why do the very people who say Jewish believers have turned their backs on their Jewish identity want to prevent them from expressing Jewish identity?

•If Jesus is not the Messiah, why does there seem to be so much fear that other Jews will believe in him, unless they are taught that to do so means being stripped of their Jewish identity?

•In a day and age when being Jewish means different things to different people, why is Jesus considered the dividing line between what is Jewish and what is not?

Jewish Believers in Jesus: Problem Children?

Jews who believe in Jesus are often described as products of unhappy, broken homes or as those who are too young, too old or too dull to exercise the mental acuity necessary to make a valid choice. Articles in Jewish newspapers routinely portray Jewish believers in Jesus as deeply troubled, vulnerable individuals with poor Jewish upbringings and little religious education.

Those allegations may be true of some Jews (and others) who believe in Jesus to the same extent that they may be true of some Jews (and others) who do not believe in Jesus. But on what basis can it be said that they are true of all, or even most, Jewish believers? Furthermore, on what basis can it be said that those are the reasons they have chosen Jesus?

We know of no evidence to show that Jews who believe in Jesus do so only because they fall into misfit categories. In fact, evidence suggests the opposite.

In 1982, Jews for Jesus conducted a survey of Jews who believe in Jesus (referred to as group B). Out of the 8,000 polled, 1,014 replied. A comparison was then made with statistics for the general Jewish popu-

28

lation (referred to as group A). The study highlighted similarities and differences between groups A and B, including age, education, and family background.

Age Composition

1982 statistics

Age	General Jewish Population (A)	Messianic Jews (B)
15-24	24%	10%
25-44	33%	72%
65+	14%	4%

Education

1982 statistics

Education	General Jewish Population (A)	Messianic Jews (B)
not completed high school	15.6%	4%
college graduates	14.2%	28%
graduate work	18.2%	23%

Jewish Observance

1982 statistics

Traditional in Jewish Observance (A)		Traditional Observance-Messianic Jews (B)	
Reformed	9.5%	all the time	40%
Conservative	34.8%	sometimes	35%
Orthodox	75.6%	not at all	25%

As you can see, 24 percent of group A, but only 10 percent of group B was in the 15–24 age bracket. At the other end of the spectrum, 14 percent of A but only 4 percent of B was 65 and over. Most Jewish believers in Jesus clustered in the young adult range, which negates the false allegations of some that "the vulnerable young and old" are especially "targeted" by Jewish people who tell them about Jesus.

In regard to education, please notice that whereas 15.6 percent of A had not completed high school, only 4 percent of B fell into that category. Group B had a higher percentage of college graduates and also a higher percentage of those who had completed post-graduate work. The survey showed that Jewish believers in Jesus were not under-educated; on the contrary, they tended to have a bit more education than their counterparts.

What about Jewish observance? In A, 9.5 percent of Reform, 34.8 percent of Conservative, and 75.6 percent of Orthodox were traditional in religious observance of Jewish holidays, Sabbath and keeping kosher. Among B, 40 percent celebrated Jewish holidays all the time, 35 percent sometimes, and 25 percent not at all. This is not an exact comparison, because group A used a more detailed yardstick to record separate statistics for various observances. Yet it can be seen that most Jewish believers in Jesus do express their sense of Jewish identity by engaging in Jewish observances.

More recent data shows that the 1982 trends demonstrated for Jewish believers in Jesus have not changed much.

You can see that figures from the 1992 Jewish American Yearbook indicate that in 1990 the median age of the Jewish core (group A) was 37.3 years. Nineteen percent of the American Jewish population was under age 15, 10.9 percent fell between the ages of 15–24, 17.6 percent fell between the ages of 25–34, 14.9 percent fell between the ages of 35–44,

19.5 percent fell between the ages of 45–64, 17.2 percent were 65 or older and 8 percent were 75 and older.

Age Composition

1992 statistics

Age	General Jewish Population (A)		Age	Messianic Jews (B)
under 15	19%		under 20	1%
15-24	10.9%		20-29	12%
25-34	17.6%		30-39	34%
35-44	14.9%		40-49	31%
45-64	19.5%		50-59	10%
65+	17.2%		60-69	6%
75+	8%		69+	5%

Notice that regarding education, 27.7 percent of group A had completed high school or less, 19.3 percent had completed some college, 26.7 percent had graduated from college and 26 percent had done graduate work.

Education

1992 statistics

Education	General Jewish Population (A)		Education	Messianic Jews (B)
high school or less	27.7%		less 12 years	4%
some college	19.3%		13 years	9%
graduated college	26.7%		14 years	15%
graduate work	26%		15 years	6%
			16 years	28%
			17 years	4%
			18 years	8%
			19 years	4%
			19 years and up	4%

In terms of observance, in the very broadest terms, 48 percent of group A observed Jewish holidays, 20 percent observed sometimes, and 32 percent did not observe Jewish holidays at all.

Jewish Observance

1992 statistics

Jewish Observance	General Jewish Population (A)	Messianic Jews (B)
observe	48%	37%
sometimes	20%	37%
don't observe	18.2%	26%

If you'll look at the 1992 update of the Jews for Jesus survey, you'll see that 1 percent of Jewish believers in Jesus who responded were under the age of 20, 12 percent were between the ages of 20–29, 34 percent were between the ages of 30–39, 31 percent were between the ages of 40–49, 10 percent were between the ages of 50–59, 6 percent were between the ages of 60–69, and 5 percent were over the age of 69.

Regarding education, note that 4 percent of group B had completed less than 12 years of school, 18 percent had 12 years, 9 percent had 13 years of school, 15 percent had 14 years and 6 percent had 15 years. Twenty-eight percent of group B had completed 16 years, 4 percent had 17 years, 8 percent had 18 years of school, 4 percent had 19 years and another 4 percent had more than 19 years of school.

Regarding holiday observance, 37 percent observed Jewish holidays, 37 percent sometimes observed them and 26 percent said they never did.

As you can see, the statistics of Jews who believe in Jesus are fairly consistent with those who don't in terms of education and holiday observance.

A Clinical Study

As a point of comparison, another study was under-taken by Jon Siegel, a Jewish person who is not a believer in Jesus. He compiled his research for a 1987 dissertation at the California School of Professional Psychology. The object of the study was "to identify differences in types of depression . . . and levels of object representation in main-stream American Jewish males and converted males of the group 'Jews for Jesus' in the age group 20–35."[22] (The phrase *object representation* is a somewhat outdated one regarding the development of relational skills and awareness.)

Siegel hypothesized that the Jews for Jesus would show higher levels of depression and that this would be due to lower levels of object representation.[23] However, the results of his study did not validate his theory. He concluded, "That my clinical impressions are quite contrary to my original hypotheses indicates the wisdom of using research to explore theory. Indications of clinical pathology in the study sample appear to have occurred with more or less the same frequency as in the Jewish sample and probably with the same frequency as in the population at large."[24]

Siegel is not a fan of Jewish believers in Jesus, and he suggested that his findings might have been due to limitations and problems in the study itself. Yet he reiterated that he was not able to substantiate any psychological difference between Jewish believers in Jesus and other Jews in his study. The fact that Siegel was obviously hoping to prove a negative point makes his admission that his theory was unsubstantiated all the more credible.

Could it be that those who have freely hypothe-sized and never tested their hypotheses have misrepresented Jewish believers in Jesus? Could it be that

the profile of the self-hating, unethical or education-
ally/intellectually/emotionally impaired Jewish
believer in Y'shua is an untested, unproved and
invalid theory?

Might it even be that we Jewish believers in Jesus
stand accused, not because of who we are, but in
order to keep other Jewish people from hearing the
message of Y'shua?

Sometimes it appears that the object of the highly
emotional articles we often read in Jewish newspapers
is not to present facts but to generate anger and fear.
That anger and fear seem intended to keep other Jews
from considering Y'shua. But doesn't this come dangerously close to emotional blackmail? Shouldn't people be free to consider who Jesus is according to
Scripture, rather than be made to feel that they, too,
will become unacceptable in the Jewish community if
they consider him with an open heart?

Time to React

When you hear a statement about Jesus such as the
preceeding ones, do you feel angry or upset? If so, we
challenge you to stop for a moment to consider the
possibility that you may be caught in the net of objections, immobilized by issues unrelated to Jesus. You
can remain bound by those objections, committed to
refusing any serious consideration of Jesus because of
everything that can be said against "the Christians."
If you choose not to know anything beyond those
objections, realize that you have made that choice,
and please consider that if it is the wrong choice, you
may some day be accountable to God for it.

Perhaps you now understand that the net of objections does not really connect with who Jesus is, what
he claimed and what he might be asking of you. You

can choose to step through any number of holes in the net. Others have done so. Leaving those objections behind does not mean that you have accepted Jesus as your Messiah. It just means that you realize that it is important for you to find out if he is. It means that some of the reasons why you have not believed are no longer enough to keep your mind closed. You want to step away, not from people you care about, but from objections some have raised that you can no longer share.

What Jewish Believers Say

The message of Jewish believers in Jesus is not who **we** are, but who **Jesus** is. Here is what just a few Jewish believers have to say about who he is and what he has meant to them. These quotes come from *Testimonies of Jews Who Believe in Jesus*[25]:

"What a revelation it was to learn that Jesus was not the personal property of the Vatican. He is ours, too, a Jew of Jews! . . . The Scriptures said that I could be a part of God's kingdom and that was the best news I had ever heard."—Norman Buskin[26]

"I had openly confessed to myself . . . and to God that I believed Jesus is the Messiah. It was like an explosion. There was a burst of light in my soul as the deeper, higher, purer power of God outweighed all my fears.

"I hadn't been able to answer the question, 'If Jesus is the Messiah, what will that mean to me?' Now I knew why. It was a question that God would answer for me moment by moment, for the rest of my life. . . . None of the repercussions I could imagine would take away the union with God that had been made possible through the Messiah Jesus."— Stan Telchin[27]

"Do we need to protect ourselves against the 'disgrace' of becoming Jews who believe in Jesus? Should we keep a chain on the door of our hearts so we don't have to see if he is out there, if he is real? No, for if Jesus is the Messiah it is no disgrace for a Jew to believe."—Vera Schlamm, M.D.[28]

"Though I didn't know it at the time, it [accepting Jesus as Messiah] was the most important decision of my life. I discovered that through Jesus, I could have the intimacy with God that our ancestors wrote about in the Tanach. As I learned more about God, he became more and more important to me. Through recent troubles, I learned to prize my relationship with him above all else. And though I still cannot explain the evil in the world, I do know the goodness and mercy I've found in God."— Scott Rubin[29]

"I'd always believed that God was somewhere 'out there' for me. It had never occurred to me that I might be here for him. . . . My old idea of a God who was there just to hand out whatever good things I might want suddenly seemed inappropriate. . . . The fact that God loved me and had suffered the hurt and humiliation of coming in flesh to redeem me made sense in light of the many [Jewish] Scriptures I'd heard over the past few months. . . . I, Laura Wertheim, the 'last holdout' in our immediate family, accepted Jesus as my Messiah."—Laura Wertheim[30]

We believe that he is the bridge, the only one who can span the gap between God who is holy, and humankind, which falls far short of God's holiness. Just as the High Priest made sacrifices for the sin of the entire nation of Israel on Yom Kippur, so we believe that Jesus not only made a sacrifice, but was the sacrifice that had previously been symbolized by the blood of innocent animals. Y'shua took our place in a way that the animals could not, and this put an end to the shedding of blood forever. He made atonement for sin and a personal relationship with God a reality for any Jew or gentile who is willing to accept it.

Perhaps you have difficulty knowing whether or not to accept that; yet you know you cannot accept the standard objections to Jesus' followers as grounds to dismiss Jesus altogether. You might feel strangely drawn to Y'shua, yet you still have a host of other questions—objections you've heard and have not been able to answer. If you are willing to hear more about Y'shua, please indicate how we may help you on the back flap of this booklet.

If you already know about Y'shua, and this booklet has helped relieve those last nagging doubts, perhaps you are ready to accept his challenge and become his person. If that is true, you can make that commitment by praying the prayer on the back flap of this booklet.

Whatever you choose to do, it is our prayer that God will bless you and give you his peace, through the Prince of Peace, Y'shua.

Endnotes:

1. Troki was a Karaite scholar. The Karaites comprise a Jewish sect that rejected the authority of the Talmud and relied solely on the Hebrew Scriptures as the source of religious authority. Though this sect has been rejected by mainstream Jewish leaders, Troki's work was widely accepted. His arguments expounding the weaknesses of Christianity were circulated and modified to the point where it would be difficult to say exactly how much of today's manuscript was in Troki's original.

2. The larger text of *The Y'shua Challenge* includes a documented essay, "That Man Jesus," on who Jesus claimed to be.

3. "Son of Man" is a title that Jesus used of himself. It is found in the Hebrew Scriptures in Daniel 7, where it refers to a heavenly messianic figure.

4. See Luke 22.

5. As it is written in the Prophets: "Behold, I send my messenger before your face, who will prepare your way before you" — "The voice of one crying in the wilderness: `Prepare the way of the Lord, make his paths straight.'" John came baptizing in the wilderness and preaching a baptism of repentance for the remission of sins. And all the land of Judea, and those from Jerusalem, went out to him and were baptized by him in the Jordan River, confessing their sins. (Mark 1:2–5)

6. Samuel Levine, *You Take Jesus, I'll Take God: How to Refute Christian Missionaries* (Los Angeles: Hamoroh Press, 1980), p. 39.

7. Hyam Maccoby, *The Mythmaker: Paul and teh Invention of Christianity* (London: Weidenfeld & Nicolson, 1986).

8. See F. F. Bruce, Paul: *Apostle of the Heart Set Free* (Grand Rapids, MI: Eerdmans, 1977), pp. 42–43.

9. Ibid., p. 50 n. 30.

10. Mishnah Sotah 9:15.

11. See Acts 16:1–4.

12. Anti-missionaries, or counter missionaries as they sometimes prefer to be called, believe it is their responsibility to prevent Jewish people from believing in Jesus. Beth Moshe, *Judaism's Truth Answers the Missionaries* (New York: Bloch Publishing Company, 1987), p. 212.

13. David Daube, *The New Testament and Rabbinic Judaism* (Salem, NH: Ayer Company, Publishers, Inc., 1992), p. 336–341.

14. Moishe Rosen, "Am Yisrael Chai," *Issues* 9:4 (1993), p. 2.

15. In Jewish religious law, it is technically impossible for a Jew (born to a Jewish mother or properly converted to Judaism) to change his religion. Even though a Jew undergoes the rites of admission to another religious faith and formally renounces the Jewish religion he remains—as far as the Halakhah is concerned—a Jew, albeit a sinner (Sanh. 44a). . . . For the born Jew, Judaism is not a matter of choice. *Encyclopedia Judaica*, Vol. 3, page 211.

16. See Luke 22:15–20.

17. Arthur I. Waskow, *The Freedom Seder: A New Haggadah for Passover* (New York; Holt, Rinehart, Winston, 1970).

18. Karen G. R. Roekard, *The Santa Cruz Haggadah: A Passover Haggadah, Coloring Book, and Journal for the Evolving Consciousness* (Capitola, CA: The Hineni Consciousness Press, 1992).

19. W. Gunther Plaut, *The Magen David: How the Six-Pointed Star Became an Emblem for the Jewish People* (Washington, D.C.: B'nai B'rith Books, 1991), p. 34.

20. Quoted in ibid., p. 36.

21. Though his stated reasons also had to do with the origins of the symbol; cf. ibid. p. 36.

22. Jon Siegel, "Depression and Level of Self and Object Representation in Minority Group Religious Converts: Jews and the 'Jews for Jesus,'" Ph.D. Dissertation, California School of Professional Psychology, 1987, p. 8.

23. Ibid, pp. 8–9.

24. Ibid., p. 91.

25. Ruth Rosen, ed., *Testimonies of Jews Who Believe in Jesus*, San Francisco: Purple Pomegranate Productions, 1987.

26. Ibid,. p. 30.

27. Ibid., p. 122.

28. Ibid., p. 153.

29. Ibid., p. 239.

30. Ibid., p. 250, 251.

Maybe you want to discover more about Y'shua.
If so, the following materials are available through Purple
Pomegranate Productions:

Paperback Books

Y'shua: The Jewish Way to Say Jesus
by Moishe Rosen...$4.95

Testimonies of Jews Who Believe in Jesus
edited by Ruth Rosen..$5.95

Christ in the Passover
by Ceil and Moishe Rosen.......................................$5.95

The Universe Is Broken: Who On Earth Can Fix It
by Moishe Rosen...$2.95

Questions and Answers From Jews for Jesus.........$1.95

Cassette Tape

The Jewish Case for Jesus
(Music and Drama)..$5.95

Publication

Issues
(A bi-monthly, eight-page, four-color mini-magazine)
                    If interested, please inquire

Some Issues *articles are available in Russian upon request.*

Send Your Materials Orders to:
Purple Pomegranate Productions
80 Page Street
San Francisco, CA 94102

Purple Pomegranate Productions
is a division of Jews for Jesus.